THE CHALLENGER

An Insight to the Enneagram 8

Asa Eccleston Kibilski

CONTENTS

MEET THE CHALLENGER: UNVEILING THE ENNEAGRAM 8'S DRIVE AND POWER

If you've ever been described as a force of nature, a trailblazer, or someone who commands a room the moment you enter, you might just be an Enneagram 8. Known as "The Challenger," type 8 individuals are a unique blend of strength, intensity, and an unwavering drive for autonomy. This is the type that isn't afraid to take charge, fight for what they believe in, and push the boundaries of what's possible. But beneath this assertive exterior lies a complex personality with a rich inner world, one that's often misunderstood or oversimplified.

In this book, we're going to dive deep into the Enneagram 8's psyche, exploring their motivations, fears, strengths, and challenges. We'll uncover the roots of their powerful energy, their yearning for control, and their underlying desire for justice and fairness. Whether you're an 8 yourself, or you're in a relationship with one, this journey will offer valuable insights and tools for understanding this dynamic and influential personality type.

The Essence of the Challenger

At their core, 8s are driven by a potent life force that compels them to make their mark on the world. They possess an innate sense of power and a deep-seated belief in their ability to shape their own destiny. This is not a type that sits passively on the sidelines; they are doers, initiators, and leaders who crave autonomy and independence. Their energy is often magnetic and contagious, drawing others into their orbit and inspiring them to take action.

Think of the 8 as a roaring fire – intense, passionate, and radiating warmth. But like any fire, they can be both destructive and creative. If their energy is unchecked, it can manifest as aggression, domination, or a ruthless pursuit of power. However, when harnessed and channeled constructively, it can fuel remarkable achievements, drive positive change, and inspire others to reach their full potential.

The 8's Superpowers (and Kryptonite)

One of the most striking qualities of the 8 is their unwavering confidence and self-assuredness. They often possess a natural charisma and an ability to command respect without even trying. Their decisiveness, directness, and willingness to take risks make them effective leaders and problem-solvers. They have a knack for cutting through the noise and getting straight to the heart of the matter, a trait that can be invaluable in high-pressure situations.

But like any superhero, the 8 has vulnerabilities. Beneath their tough exterior, they often harbor a fear of being controlled or betrayed. This can lead to an overemphasis on self-reliance, a reluctance to show vulnerability, and a tendency to push others away. They may struggle with intimacy and emotional expression, preferring to maintain control over their feelings.

Understanding the Enneagram 8's Worldview

To truly understand the Enneagram 8, we must explore their unique worldview. They see the world as a place where power dynamics are constantly at play, and they are determined to be in control of their own narrative. They value strength, honesty, and authenticity, and they have little patience for weakness, deception, or injustice.

Their strong sense of justice often drives them to become advocates for the underdog, standing up to bullies and fighting for the rights of others. But their desire for control can sometimes lead to an "ends justify the means" mentality, where they may bend the rules or disregard the feelings of others in pursuit of their goals.

The Journey Ahead

In the following chapters, we'll delve deeper into the complexities of the Enneagram 8, exploring their relationships, their careers, and their spiritual paths. We'll examine their strengths and weaknesses, their triggers and growth opportunities. We'll also provide practical tools and strategies for 8s to harness their power, cultivate healthier relationships, and live more fulfilling lives. So buckle up, because this is going to be an exhilarating ride!

CENTERS OF INTELLIGENCE: HOW GUT, HEART, AND HEAD SHAPE THE 8'S EXPERIENCE

The Enneagram isn't just about identifying your personality type. It's a rich and insightful framework for understanding how our minds, hearts, and bodies interact to shape our experience of the world. At the heart of this framework lies the concept of the three centers of intelligence: the Gut (Instinctual), the Heart (Emotional), and the Head (Mental). Each of us has a dominant center that influences how we perceive, process, and respond to information. For the Enneagram 8, the gut center reigns supreme, but their heart and head centers play crucial roles as well.

The Gut Center: The 8's Powerhouse

As a gut-centered type, the 8 is deeply connected to their instincts and intuition. They are highly attuned to their physical sensations and visceral reactions, often making decisions based on what feels right in their gut. This is the source of their incredible drive, energy, and willpower. When an 8 sets their mind on something, they are unstoppable.

The gut center is also the 8's primary defense mechanism. They use their instincts to assess threats and protect themselves from perceived harm. This can manifest as a strong need for control, a quick temper, or a tendency to push others away when they feel vulnerable.

For the 8, power is not just about external dominance; it's about feeling safe and secure in a world that can often feel unpredictable and threatening. They seek control over their environment and relationships to avoid feeling vulnerable or powerless.

The Heart Center: The 8's Hidden Depths

While the gut center dominates, the heart center holds significant power for the 8. It's where their deepest desires, passions, and fears reside. Eights often have a strong sense of loyalty and protectiveness towards those they care about. They can be incredibly generous and supportive, willing to go to great lengths to help their loved ones.

However, accessing their heart center can be challenging for the 8. They may suppress their emotions to maintain control, leading to a build-up of anger, resentment, or anxiety. They may also struggle with vulnerability and intimacy, fearing that opening up will make them weak or susceptible to manipulation.

Learning to connect with their heart center is crucial for the 8's growth and well-being. It allows them to experience a wider range of emotions, cultivate deeper relationships, and develop greater compassion for themselves and others.

The Head Center: The 8's Strategic Mind

The head center provides the 8 with their strategic thinking abilities, their knack for problem-solving, and their drive for justice and fairness. Eights often possess a sharp intellect and a quick wit. They enjoy analyzing situations, planning their next moves, and strategizing to achieve their goals.

However, the 8's head center can also be a source of challenges. Their need for control can lead to overthinking, micromanaging, and a tendency to bulldoze over others' opinions. They may also become rigid in their thinking, clinging to their beliefs even when presented with new information.

Learning to balance their head center with their gut and heart centers is essential for the 8's personal development. It allows them to become more flexible, open-minded, and collaborative, while still maintaining their decisive and action-oriented nature.

Integrating the Centers

The Enneagram 8's journey towards growth involves integrating their gut, heart, and head centers. By acknowledging and embracing all aspects of themselves, they can become more self-aware, compassionate, and effective in their relationships and endeavors.

In the following chapters, we'll delve deeper into each center of intelligence, exploring how it influences the 8's behavior, relationships, and worldview. We'll also provide practical tools and strategies for the 8 to cultivate greater balance and harmony among their centers, leading to a more fulfilling and authentic life.

THE WINGS OF INFLUENCE: UNDERSTANDING THE 8W7 (ADVENTURER) AND 8W9 (PEACEMAKER)

As we delve further into the world of the Enneagram 8, it's important to recognize that not all Challengers are created equal. While they share the core motivations and characteristics of their type, each individual 8 is shaped by their unique experiences, values, and, crucially, their wing. A "wing" in Enneagram terms refers to the type that's adjacent to your core type on the Enneagram circle. For Eights, this means they can either have a 7 wing (8w7) or a 9 wing (8w9).

The influence of a wing can be significant, adding a distinct flavor and nuance to the core 8 personality. Understanding your wing can provide valuable insights into your strengths, challenges, and potential areas for growth. Let's explore the two wings of the Enneagram 8 and discover how they shape the Challenger's journey.

The 8w7 (Adventurer): High-Octane Energy and a Thirst for Experience

Imagine the Enneagram 8 as a powerful engine, and the 7 wing as the nitrous oxide booster. The 8w7 is a whirlwind of energy, enthusiasm, and a relentless pursuit of excitement. They are the life of the party, the daredevils, the ones always seeking new adventures and experiences.

With their 7 wing, 8w7s are naturally charismatic and optimistic. They exude confidence and charm, drawing others into their orbit with their infectious energy. They are quick-witted, spontaneous, and always up for a good time. Their natural leadership abilities are amplified by their ability to inspire and motivate others with their positive outlook.

However, the 8w7's boundless energy can also be their Achilles' heel. They may struggle with impulsivity, restlessness, and a tendency to overextend themselves. Their desire for constant stimulation can lead to a fear of missing out (FOMO) and a difficulty staying focused on one thing for too long.

The 8w9 (Peacemaker): Calm Strength and a Desire for Harmony

While the 8w7 is a force of nature, the 8w9 is more like a gentle giant. They possess a calm strength and a grounded presence that can be both reassuring and intimidating. Their 9 wing tempers the 8's intensity, bringing a desire for peace, harmony, and connection.

8w9s are natural mediators and peacemakers. They have a knack for diffusing conflict and finding common ground. They are often more diplomatic and tactful than their 8w7 counterparts, preferring to avoid confrontation when possible. Their calm demeanor and ability to see multiple perspectives make them excellent leaders and negotiators.

However, the 8w9's desire for harmony can sometimes lead to a tendency to avoid conflict altogether, even when it's necessary to address an issue. They may also struggle with expressing their anger or asserting their needs, fearing that it will disrupt the peace.

Embracing Your Wing

Understanding your wing is a key step in your Enneagram journey. It can help you identify your unique strengths and challenges, as well as potential areas for growth.

If you're an 8w7, you can learn to harness your boundless energy and enthusiasm while also developing greater focus and discipline. You can learn to channel your spontaneity into creative projects and use your charisma to inspire others.

If you're an 8w9, you can learn to embrace your calm strength and use your diplomatic skills to build bridges and resolve conflicts. You can also learn to assert your needs and express your anger in healthy ways.

Remember, your wing is not a limitation, but rather a potential asset. By recognizing and embracing your wing's influence, you can become a more well-rounded and effective 8.

In the following chapters, we'll explore the specific ways in which each wing influences the 8's experience in different areas of life, including relationships, career, and personal growth. We'll also provide practical tools and strategies for each wing to leverage their strengths and overcome their challenges. So whether you're an 8w7 or an 8w9, get ready to discover the full potential of your Challenger spirit.

THE GUT TRIAD: NAVIGATING POWER DYNAMICS WITH TYPES 8, 9, AND 1

The Enneagram is not just a collection of nine distinct personality types; it's a map of interconnected relationships and dynamics. Each type belongs to a triad, a group of three types that share a common emotional center and a particular way of relating to the world. The Enneagram 8, along with types 9 and 1, belongs to the gut triad. This triad is characterized by a focus on instinctual energy, a concern for justice and control, and a powerful emotional response to perceived threats or injustices.

Understanding the dynamics of the gut triad can provide invaluable insights into the 8's relationships with others, particularly with 9s and 1s. It can help illuminate the potential for conflict, as well as opportunities for growth and collaboration.

The Gut Triad's Common Ground: Instinct, Action, and Intensity

All three types in the gut triad share a deep connection to their instincts and a tendency to act on their gut feelings. They are driven by a strong sense of inner knowing and often make decisions based on what feels right in their body rather than rational analysis. This shared instinctual energy can create a powerful bond between members of the gut triad, as they can often understand and appreciate each other's directness, decisiveness, and willingness to take action.

However, this same intensity can also lead to clashes, especially when their instincts and values conflict. The 8's assertiveness may feel overwhelming to the 9's desire for peace, while the 1's focus on rules and principles may clash with the 8's tendency to bend the rules.

8 and 9: The Powerhouse and the Peacemaker

The relationship between 8s and 9s can be a fascinating dance of opposites. The 8's bold energy and assertive nature can be both attractive and intimidating to the 9, who often seeks a calm and harmonious environment. The 9's gentle demeanor and ability to go with the flow can provide a soothing counterbalance to the 8's intensity, helping them to relax and connect with their softer side.

However, the 8 may also see the 9 as passive or indecisive, while the 9 may feel overwhelmed or controlled by the 8's forceful personality. To navigate this dynamic successfully, both types need to cultivate empathy and understanding. The 8 needs to learn to tone down their intensity and respect the 9's need for peace, while the 9 needs to learn to assert their needs and not allow themselves to be steamrolled by the 8.

8 and 1: The Challenger and the Reformer

The relationship between 8s and 1s is often characterized by a mutual respect for strength and a shared desire for justice. Both types are driven by a strong moral compass and a willingness to fight for what they believe in. They can be powerful allies in causes they care about, using their combined energy and passion to create positive change.

However, their differing approaches to achieving their goals can create friction. The 8's tendency to bend the rules and take shortcuts may clash with the 1's strict adherence to principles and procedures. The 1 may also see the 8 as overly aggressive or impulsive, while the 8 may view the 1 as rigid and inflexible.

To build a successful relationship, both types need to appreciate each other's strengths and respect their differences. The 8 needs to learn to value the 1's attention to detail and commitment to ethical behavior, while the 1 needs to learn to appreciate the 8's ability to take action and get things done.

The Gut Triad's Potential for Growth

The gut triad offers a unique opportunity for personal growth and transformation. By understanding and appreciating the strengths and challenges of each type, members of the gut triad can learn from each other and develop a more holistic and balanced approach to life.

For the 8, learning to connect with their heart center and cultivate empathy can help them to temper their intensity and build more fulfilling relationships. Embracing the 9's calmness and the 1's attention to detail can also help the 8 to become more patient, compassionate, and effective in their endeavors.

By recognizing the interconnectedness of the gut triad, we can begin to unravel the complex dynamics that shape our relationships and our lives. Through understanding and acceptance, we can learn to harness the power of the gut triad to create positive change and build a more just and harmonious world.

INSTINCTUAL SUBTYPES: HOW SELF-PRESERVATION, SOCIAL, AND SEXUAL INSTINCTS DRIVE THE 8

While the Enneagram 8's gut-centered nature is a defining characteristic, there's another layer of complexity that adds depth and nuance to their personality – the instinctual subtypes. These subtypes, also known as instinctual variants, are rooted in our primal survival instincts and represent how we prioritize our basic needs and interact with the world.

Each of the nine Enneagram types can manifest in three distinct instinctual subtypes:

1. **Self-Preservation (SP):** Focused on securing basic needs like safety, resources, and well-being.
2. **Social (SO):** Concerned with belonging, social status, and contributing to the group.
3. **Sexual (SX):** Driven by intensity, intimacy, and a craving for stimulating experiences.

Each of us has all three instincts, but one tends to be dominant, influencing our behavior, priorities, and relationships. Understanding your dominant instinctual subtype can shed light on your core motivations, fears, and desires, providing a more comprehensive picture of your Enneagram 8 personality.

The Self-Preservation 8 (SP8): The Fortress Builder

The SP8 is the most grounded and practical of the three 8 subtypes. Their primary concern is ensuring their survival and well-being, both physically and materially. They are often driven to accumulate resources, build a secure foundation for themselves and their loved ones, and protect themselves from perceived threats.

SP8s are typically hardworking, responsible, and resourceful. They have a strong work ethic and a knack for managing finances and practical matters. They may also be drawn to careers that offer stability and security, such as law enforcement, the military, or business.

However, the SP8's focus on self-preservation can also manifest as a tendency towards hoarding, excessive control, and a fear of scarcity. They may struggle with trusting others or delegating tasks, as they feel a strong need to be self-sufficient and in control of their environment.

The Social 8 (SO8): The Group Leader

The SO8 is the most outwardly focused of the three 8 subtypes. They are deeply concerned with their social status and their role within the group. They are often natural leaders, drawn to positions of power and influence. They thrive on making a difference in the world and leaving their mark on society.

SO8s are typically charismatic, persuasive, and influential. They have a knack for rallying others around a common cause and inspiring them to take action. They may also be drawn to careers in politics, activism, or social entrepreneurship.

However, the SO8's focus on social status can also manifest as a need for approval and recognition, a fear of rejection, and a tendency to dominate or control others. They may also struggle with intimacy and vulnerability, preferring to maintain a strong and confident facade.

The Sexual 8 (SX8): The Intensity Seeker

The SX8 is the most passionate and intense of the three 8 subtypes. They are driven by a craving for deep connection, intimacy, and stimulating experiences. They are often drawn to relationships that are passionate, adventurous, and emotionally charged.

SX8s are typically charismatic, magnetic, and alluring. They have a powerful presence and an ability to captivate others with their intensity and passion. They may also be drawn to careers in the arts, entertainment, or fields that allow for creative self-expression.

However, the SX8's intensity can also manifest as a possessiveness, jealousy, and a fear of abandonment. They may also struggle with emotional regulation and a tendency to create drama or conflict in their relationships.

Unveiling Your Instinctual Subtype

Identifying your dominant instinctual subtype can provide a deeper understanding of your motivations, fears, and desires. It can also help you to navigate relationships, choose a fulfilling career path, and cultivate greater self-awareness.

To discover your subtype, pay attention to your patterns of behavior, your priorities, and your reactions to stress. Consider which of the three instincts feels most essential to your well-being and which one you tend to prioritize in your daily life.

Remember, your subtype is not a fixed label but rather a dynamic aspect of your personality. By understanding your dominant instinct, you can learn to harness its power while also managing its potential challenges.

THE HEART'S ARMOR: THE 8'S RELATIONSHIP WITH VULNERABILITY AND ANGER

The Enneagram 8, the bold and assertive Challenger, is often associated with strength, power, and an unwavering determination. Their gut-centered nature fuels their drive and passion, propelling them to take charge, overcome obstacles, and make their mark on the world. But beneath this formidable exterior lies a heart that is both fierce and tender, a heart that yearns for connection and intimacy but often struggles with vulnerability and emotional expression.

The 8's relationship with their heart center is a complex and often paradoxical one. On one hand, they are deeply passionate and caring individuals, fiercely loyal to their loved ones and fiercely protective of those they consider their own. On the other hand, they often build a fortress around their heart, fearing that vulnerability will make them weak and susceptible to harm.

The Armor of Strength

This protective armor is often forged in early childhood experiences, where the 8 may have learned that showing vulnerability leads to pain and betrayal. To shield themselves from further hurt, they develop a tough exterior, a persona of strength and invincibility. They learn to suppress their emotions, deny their need for others, and project an image of self-reliance and control.

This armor serves them well in many ways. It allows them to navigate a world that can often feel hostile and unpredictable. It protects them from emotional pain and gives them the confidence to take risks and pursue their goals. But like any armor, it also restricts their movement and limits their ability to fully connect with themselves and others.

The Challenge of Vulnerability

For the 8, vulnerability is often equated with weakness. They fear that showing their soft underbelly will expose them to attack or manipulation. They may also struggle with expressing their emotions, preferring to bottle them up or channel them into anger or action.

This reluctance to show vulnerability can create a barrier in their relationships. It can make it difficult for them to form deep and meaningful connections with others. They may also struggle to ask for help or support, preferring to shoulder their burdens alone.

However, vulnerability is not a weakness. It is a strength, a sign of courage and authenticity. It is the key to building trust, intimacy, and deeper connections with others. For the 8, learning to embrace vulnerability is a crucial step towards personal growth and fulfillment.

Anger: The 8's Double-Edged Sword

Anger is a complex and often misunderstood emotion. For the Enneagram 8, anger is both a shield and a weapon. It can be a powerful motivator, fueling their drive for justice and fairness. It can also be a way to mask their vulnerability, to project an image of strength and control.

However, anger can also be destructive. When left unchecked, it can lead to aggression, resentment, and strained relationships. It can also take a toll on the 8's physical and mental health.

Learning to manage anger is a crucial step for the 8's personal development. It involves recognizing the triggers that set off their anger, developing healthy coping mechanisms, and learning to express their emotions in constructive ways.

The Path to Emotional Liberation

For the Enneagram 8, the journey towards emotional liberation involves learning to embrace vulnerability and manage anger in healthy ways. It involves recognizing that strength and vulnerability are not mutually exclusive, but rather complementary qualities. It involves learning to trust others, to open up their heart, and to allow themselves to be seen and loved for who they truly are.

This is not an easy path, but it is a rewarding one. By embracing their heart center, the 8 can discover a whole new dimension to their being. They can experience deeper love, more fulfilling relationships, and a greater sense of peace and wholeness.

THE COUNTER-PHOBIC STANCE: FACING FEAR HEAD-ON (AND WHY IT'S CRUCIAL)

In the grand tapestry of the Enneagram 8, a unique pattern emerges – a paradox known as the "counter-phobic stance." It's a captivating dance between fear and defiance, a psychological mechanism that compels Challengers to confront their fears head-on, often with a ferocity that masks their underlying anxieties.

At first glance, this might seem counterintuitive. Aren't Eights supposed to be fearless, the ones who charge into battle without a second thought? While their boldness and assertiveness are undeniable, the truth is more nuanced. Eights, like everyone else, experience fear. But their way of dealing with it sets them apart.

The Anatomy of the Counter-Phobic Stance

The counter-phobic stance is a defense mechanism rooted in the 8's deep-seated fear of vulnerability and powerlessness. When confronted with a situation that triggers these fears, instead of retreating or withdrawing, the 8 does the opposite. They lean in, taking aggressive action to assert their control and dispel their anxiety.

This can manifest in various ways:

- **Confrontation:** Instead of avoiding conflict, they may initiate it, seeking to dominate the situation and eliminate the perceived threat.
- **Denial:** They may deny their fear altogether, convincing themselves that they are not afraid, even when their body and mind are signaling otherwise.
- **Minimization:** They may downplay the significance of their

fear, brushing it off as trivial or unimportant.

- **Overcompensation:** They may act overly confident and assertive, even when feeling insecure or unsure.

While the counter-phobic stance can be an effective short-term strategy for managing fear, it's not a sustainable long-term solution. By constantly pushing their fears away, Eights risk missing out on valuable opportunities for growth and self-discovery.

The Fear Beneath the Bravado

To understand the counter-phobic stance, we must explore the fears that lie at its root. For Eights, the most primal fear is losing control. They dread the feeling of being powerless, vulnerable, or at the mercy of others. This fear can stem from childhood experiences of neglect, abuse, or betrayal.

Another common fear for Eights is being seen as weak or incapable. They strive to maintain an image of strength and self-reliance, fearing that showing vulnerability will make them targets for manipulation or exploitation.

These fears are not unfounded. Eights have often faced challenges and adversity that have forced them to develop a thick skin and a fierce independence. However, their counter-phobic stance can also create a self-fulfilling prophecy. By constantly pushing away their fears, they may inadvertently attract situations that confirm their worst fears.

The Power of Facing Fear

The counter-phobic stance is not a flaw or a weakness; it's a survival mechanism that has served Eights well in many situations. However, it's important to recognize that facing fear head-on can be a more empowering and ultimately liberating approach.

By acknowledging and accepting their fears, Eights can begin to dismantle the barriers that prevent them from fully experiencing life. They can learn to embrace vulnerability as a source of strength, rather than a weakness. They can discover that opening up to others doesn't make them less powerful, but rather more human and relatable.

Facing fear can also lead to greater self-awareness and personal growth. By understanding the root of their fears, Eights can begin to challenge their limiting beliefs and develop healthier coping mechanisms. They can learn to channel their energy into constructive action, rather than using it to mask their anxieties.

The Journey Towards Wholeness

For the Enneagram 8, the journey towards wholeness involves embracing both their strength and their vulnerability. It involves recognizing that fear is a natural part of the human experience, and that facing it head-on can lead to greater resilience, courage, and compassion.

This journey is not without its challenges. It requires a willingness to step outside of one's comfort zone, to challenge long-held beliefs, and to risk feeling vulnerable. But the rewards are immeasurable.

By facing their fears, Eights can discover a deeper sense of inner peace and fulfillment. They can develop more authentic and fulfilling relationships. They can unleash their full potential and live a life that is both powerful and compassionate.

HEALTHY EMOTIONAL EXPRESSION: FINDING BALANCE AND COMPASSION

The Enneagram 8, known for their strength, resilience, and unwavering drive, often grapples with a unique challenge: navigating the complex landscape of their emotions. Their gut-centered nature, while empowering, can also lead to a suppression of feelings, a tendency to bottle up emotions until they erupt in outbursts of anger or frustration.

However, the path to a fulfilling life for an 8 isn't about denying their emotions but rather about finding healthy ways to express and channel them. It's about discovering a balance between their natural assertiveness and a newfound capacity for vulnerability, compassion, and empathy.

The Emotional Landscape of the 8

Eights experience a wide range of emotions, just like any other Enneagram type. They feel joy, excitement, love, and grief, but they may not always express these emotions in conventional ways. Their fear of vulnerability often leads them to suppress their softer feelings, fearing that showing weakness will make them targets for manipulation or exploitation.

Anger, however, is an emotion that Eights readily express. It's a powerful force that can fuel their drive for justice and fairness, but it can also become a destructive force if left unchecked. Eights often struggle with finding healthy outlets for their anger, leading to outbursts, resentment, and strained relationships.

Unmasking the Vulnerability Beneath the Anger

It's important to understand that anger, for the 8, is often a mask for other emotions. Beneath the surface of their rage may lie hurt, fear, or sadness. When Eights feel threatened or vulnerable, their first instinct is to lash out, to protect themselves from further pain.

However, this reactive anger can create a vicious cycle. By pushing away their softer emotions, Eights deny themselves the opportunity to process and heal from their pain. This can lead to a buildup of resentment and anger, which can further isolate them from others and exacerbate their emotional struggles.

The Path to Emotional Balance

The key to emotional balance for the Enneagram 8 lies in developing a greater awareness of their emotional landscape. This involves:

1. **Recognizing and Naming Emotions:** Eights need to learn to identify and name their emotions, even the ones that feel uncomfortable or threatening. This can involve journaling, talking to a trusted friend or therapist, or simply taking a few moments to check in with themselves and ask, "What am I feeling right now?"

2. **Allowing Vulnerability:** Eights need to give themselves permission to be vulnerable, to express their softer emotions without fear of judgment or rejection. This can involve sharing their feelings with loved ones, seeking support when needed, or simply allowing themselves to cry or feel sad.

3. **Finding Healthy Outlets for Anger:** Eights need to find constructive ways to channel their anger, such as exercise, creative expression, or advocating for a cause they believe in. It's also important to learn to communicate anger in healthy ways, expressing their needs and boundaries without resorting to aggression or manipulation.

4. **Cultivating Compassion:** Eights need to develop greater compassion for themselves and others. This involves recognizing that everyone has flaws and vulnerabilities, and that it's okay to make mistakes and ask for help. It also involves learning to see the world through the eyes of others, to understand their perspectives and motivations.

The Rewards of Emotional Expression

The journey towards emotional balance is not an easy one for the Enneagram 8, but it is a rewarding one. By embracing their full range of emotions, Eights can experience a greater sense of freedom, authenticity, and connection with others. They can discover a deeper level of self-acceptance and compassion, and they can build more meaningful and fulfilling relationships.

As Eights learn to express their emotions in healthy ways, they may find that their anger subsides, their relationships improve, and their overall well-being increases. They may also discover hidden talents and passions that were previously suppressed by their fear of vulnerability.

By embracing the full spectrum of their emotional experience, Eights can tap into their true power, a power that is not based on control or dominance, but on authenticity, vulnerability, and compassion.

THE THINKING TRIAD: STRATEGIES, CONTROL, AND THE 8'S RELATIONSHIP WITH TYPES 5 AND 7

In the grand symphony of the Enneagram, each personality type plays a unique instrument, contributing to the rich tapestry of human experience. The Enneagram 8, the bold and assertive Challenger, finds themselves harmonizing with types 5 and 7 in the Thinking Triad, a trio united by their shared focus on the head center – the realm of thoughts, ideas, and strategies.

While the 8's gut-centered nature is their driving force, their head center plays a crucial role in shaping their worldview and interactions with others. This triad's common ground lies in their strategic thinking, their need for knowledge and understanding, and their tendency to analyze situations before taking action.

However, like any harmonious chord, the Thinking Triad also has its dissonances. The 8's assertive nature can clash with the 5's need for detachment and the 7's desire for freedom and excitement. Understanding these dynamics is crucial for navigating relationships and fostering personal growth within the triad.

The Thinking Triad's Common Ground: Strategy and Analysis

All three types in the Thinking Triad share a love for knowledge, a thirst for understanding, and a talent for strategic thinking. They approach life with a curious and analytical mind, constantly seeking to make sense of the world around them.

For the 8, this translates into a desire to understand power dynamics and social structures. They analyze situations to identify potential threats and opportunities, strategizing to maintain control and achieve their goals.

The 5, on the other hand, is driven by a need to accumulate knowledge and expertise. They analyze information to gain a deeper understanding of the world and protect themselves from feeling overwhelmed or unprepared.

The 7, with their insatiable curiosity, seeks to experience life to the fullest. They analyze situations to identify potential sources of fun and excitement, strategizing to avoid boredom and pain.

This shared love for strategy and analysis can create a strong intellectual connection between members of the Thinking Triad. They can engage in stimulating conversations, challenge each other's perspectives, and collaborate on projects that require careful planning and execution.

8 and 5: The Challenger and the Investigator

The relationship between 8s and 5s can be a fascinating dance of power and knowledge. The 8's assertiveness and decisiveness can be both inspiring and intimidating to the 5, who often prefers to observe and analyze from a distance. The 5's vast knowledge and analytical skills can be invaluable to the 8, helping them to refine their strategies and make informed decisions.

However, the 8 may also see the 5 as overly cautious or detached, while the 5 may feel overwhelmed by the 8's intensity and need for control. To navigate this dynamic successfully, both types need to cultivate respect for each other's strengths and weaknesses. The 8 needs to learn to appreciate the 5's intellectual depth and give them space to process information, while the 5 needs to learn to trust the 8's instincts and assertiveness.

8 and 7: The Challenger and the Enthusiast

The relationship between 8s and 7s is often characterized by a shared love for adventure and a mutual appreciation for each other's energy and enthusiasm. The 8's bold spirit and willingness to take risks can inspire the 7 to step outside their comfort zone and embrace new experiences. The 7's optimism and playful nature can help the 8 to lighten up and enjoy the present moment.

However, the 8 may also see the 7 as scattered or irresponsible, while the 7 may feel constrained by the 8's need for control and structure. To build a successful relationship, both types need to find a balance between their competing needs. The 8 needs to learn to loosen up and allow the 7 some freedom to explore, while the 7 needs to learn to respect the 8's boundaries and need for stability.

The Thinking Triad's Potential for Growth

The Thinking Triad offers a unique opportunity for personal growth and transformation. By understanding and appreciating the strengths and challenges of each type, members of the triad can learn from each other and develop a more holistic and balanced approach to life.

For the 8, learning to integrate their heart and gut centers with their head center can help them to become more compassionate, intuitive, and emotionally expressive. Embracing the 5's intellectual curiosity and the 7's enthusiasm can also help the 8 to broaden their horizons, explore new possibilities, and cultivate a greater sense of joy and wonder.

THE QUEST FOR JUSTICE:
THE 8'S MORAL COMPASS
AND DRIVE FOR FAIRNESS

At the heart of the Enneagram 8's powerful personality lies a deep-seated yearning for justice. This is not merely a theoretical concept for them; it's a visceral, gut-level imperative that fuels their actions and shapes their worldview. Their moral compass is finely tuned to detect injustice, inequality, and abuse of power, and they feel a personal responsibility to right those wrongs, to level the playing field, and to defend the underdog.

This unwavering sense of justice is both a blessing and a curse for the 8. It drives them to become passionate advocates, tireless champions for the vulnerable, and fearless leaders who challenge the status quo. But it can also lead to a black-and-white view of morality, a tendency to see the world in terms of good versus evil, and a willingness to bend or break the rules in pursuit of what they believe is right.

The Origins of the 8's Moral Compass

The 8's quest for justice is often rooted in their childhood experiences. They may have witnessed injustice or experienced unfair treatment themselves, leaving them with a deep-seated anger and a determination to prevent others from suffering the same fate.

This early exposure to injustice can shape the 8's worldview, instilling in them a belief that the world is a dangerous place where the strong prey on the weak. This belief can fuel their need for control and their desire to protect themselves and others from harm.

However, the 8's sense of justice is not merely a reaction to past trauma. It's also a reflection of their innate sense of fairness and their belief in the inherent worth and dignity of all human beings. They see the world as a place where everyone deserves a fair shot, and they are willing to fight tooth and nail to make that a reality.

The 8 as Advocate and Protector

The 8's drive for justice manifests in various ways. They may become vocal advocates for social justice causes, fighting against discrimination, inequality, and oppression. They may also take on roles as protectors, shielding the vulnerable from harm and standing up to bullies and abusers.

In the workplace, they may become whistle-blowers, exposing unethical practices or advocating for fair treatment of employees. In their personal lives, they may fiercely defend their loved ones and challenge anyone who threatens their well-being.

The 8's passion for justice is not always welcomed or appreciated. They may be seen as troublemakers, disruptors, or even bullies themselves. However, their unwavering commitment to what they believe is right often inspires others and sparks positive change.

The Dark Side of the 8's Quest for Justice

While the 8's sense of justice is a noble quality, it can also have a dark side. Their black-and-white view of morality can lead to a rigid judgment of others and a tendency to see the world in terms of good guys and bad guys.

Their desire to protect and defend can also become distorted, leading to controlling or domineering behavior. In their quest for justice, they may cross ethical boundaries or disregard the feelings of others.

It's important for Eights to recognize the potential pitfalls of their righteous indignation. While their passion for justice is admirable, they need to temper it with compassion, empathy, and a willingness to see the nuances of complex situations.

Balancing Justice with Compassion

The Enneagram 8's journey towards growth involves integrating their passion for justice with compassion and understanding. This means recognizing that not everyone shares their black-and-white view of morality, and that there are often multiple perspectives to consider.

It also means learning to channel their anger into constructive action, rather than lashing out or seeking revenge. Eights can use their powerful energy to advocate for positive change, build bridges between conflicting parties, and create a more just and equitable world.

By balancing their drive for justice with compassion, Eights can become powerful agents of change, inspiring others with their courage, conviction, and unwavering belief in a better future. They can use their strengths to fight for what they believe in while also respecting the dignity and autonomy of others.

OVERCOMING BLIND SPOTS: RECOGNIZING AND CHALLENGING ASSUMPTIONS

Enneagram 8s, with their decisive nature and unwavering confidence, are often seen as visionary leaders and powerful agents of change. Their gut-centered instincts and strategic thinking abilities allow them to navigate complex situations with ease, making decisions swiftly and confidently. However, like all Enneagram types, 8s have their blind spots, areas where their strengths can become weaknesses if not consciously managed.

In this chapter, we'll delve into the common blind spots that can hinder the 8's growth and development. We'll explore how their need for control, their aversion to vulnerability, and their tendency to see the world in black and white can sometimes lead to misunderstandings, conflicts, and missed opportunities.

The Blind Spot of Control

Eights have a natural need for control. They feel most secure when they are in charge, able to dictate the terms and direct the course of events. This need for control can be a powerful asset, driving them to achieve their goals and protect themselves from perceived threats. However, it can also become a blind spot, leading them to micromanage, dominate others, and resist change.

When Eights feel their control slipping, they may become anxious, defensive, or even aggressive. They may also struggle to delegate tasks or trust others to make decisions, fearing that they won't live up to their high standards.

To overcome this blind spot, Eights need to learn to relinquish some control and embrace a more collaborative approach. This involves recognizing that they don't have to be in charge of everything, and that allowing others to share the responsibility can actually lead to better outcomes.

The Blind Spot of Vulnerability

Eights often view vulnerability as a weakness, a chink in their armor that could be exploited by others. They may suppress their emotions, deny their need for support, and project an image of invincibility. While this strategy can protect them from emotional pain in the short term, it can also hinder their growth and prevent them from forming deeper connections with others.

When Eights refuse to acknowledge their vulnerability, they miss out on opportunities for empathy, intimacy, and self-discovery. They may also come across as cold, distant, or even arrogant, pushing away the very people they need in their lives.

To overcome this blind spot, Eights need to embrace their vulnerability as a source of strength. They need to learn to trust others, to open up about their fears and insecurities, and to allow themselves to be seen and loved for who they truly are.

The Blind Spot of Black-and-White Thinking

Eights tend to see the world in stark terms, with clear distinctions between right and wrong, good and evil. This black-and-white thinking can be helpful in situations that require decisive action, but it can also lead to rigidity, judgmentalness, and an inability to see nuances or complexities.

When Eights view the world through a black-and-white lens, they may struggle to understand differing perspectives or empathize with those who don't share their values. They may also become overly critical of themselves and others, leading to self-doubt and conflict.

To overcome this blind spot, Eights need to cultivate a more nuanced and flexible worldview. This involves recognizing that there are often multiple valid perspectives, and that situations are rarely as simple as they seem. It also involves learning to accept ambiguity and uncertainty, and to embrace the complexity of human experience.

Embracing Growth and Transformation

Recognizing and challenging our blind spots is an essential part of personal growth. For Enneagram 8s, this journey involves learning to balance their strengths with a greater awareness of their limitations. It involves embracing vulnerability, cultivating empathy, and developing a more nuanced understanding of the world.

By addressing their blind spots, Eights can tap into their full potential as leaders, advocates, and agents of change. They can use their strengths to make a positive impact on the world while also building deeper, more meaningful relationships with others.

This journey is not always easy, but it is incredibly rewarding. By overcoming their blind spots, Eights can discover a newfound sense of freedom, authenticity, and wholeness. They can live a life that is both powerful and compassionate, a life that is truly aligned with their values and their deepest desires.

INTEGRATION TO 2: LEARNING THE POWER OF VULNERABILITY AND GENEROSITY

The Enneagram is not just a tool for self-understanding; it's a map for personal growth and transformation. Each type has a path of integration, a direction they can move towards to become more balanced, whole, and fulfilled. For the Enneagram 8, the path of integration leads to type 2, the Helper. This journey involves embracing qualities that may seem counterintuitive to the 8's natural tendencies: vulnerability, empathy, and generosity.

At first glance, the 8 and the 2 may seem like polar opposites. The 8 is assertive, self-reliant, and driven by a need for control, while the 2 is warm, empathetic, and motivated by a desire to help and connect with others. However, these seemingly opposing qualities can actually complement and enhance each other, creating a more well-rounded and harmonious individual.

Embracing Vulnerability: The Key to Deeper Connection

For the 8, who often views vulnerability as a weakness, the idea of integrating to 2 can be challenging. They may fear that opening up to others will make them vulnerable to attack or manipulation. However, vulnerability is not a sign of weakness; it's a sign of courage and authenticity. It's the willingness to let down one's guard, to share one's true feelings, and to risk being hurt or rejected.

When 8s learn to embrace vulnerability, they open themselves up to a whole new world of possibilities. They can experience deeper intimacy in their relationships, connect with others on a more authentic level, and develop a greater sense of compassion for themselves and others.

Cultivating Empathy: Understanding the Needs of Others

Another key aspect of integrating to 2 is cultivating empathy, the ability to understand and share the feelings of others. Eights are often focused on their own needs and desires, and they may struggle to see things from other people's perspectives.

By developing empathy, 8s can learn to see the world through the eyes of others, to understand their motivations and emotions. This can lead to greater compassion, improved communication, and more harmonious relationships.

Practicing Generosity: Giving from the Heart

Generosity is a hallmark of the Enneagram 2, and it's a quality that can greatly benefit the 8. By learning to give freely and unconditionally, 8s can discover a new source of joy and fulfillment. They can also learn to let go of their need for control and trust that others are capable of taking care of themselves.

Generosity doesn't have to be grand gestures or extravagant gifts. It can be as simple as offering a listening ear, a helping hand, or a word of encouragement. By practicing generosity in their daily lives, 8s can cultivate a more open-hearted and compassionate approach to life.

The Integrated 8: A Powerful Force for Good

When the Enneagram 8 integrates to 2, they become a truly unstoppable force for good. Their natural strength, assertiveness, and leadership abilities are enhanced by a newfound vulnerability, empathy, and generosity. They can use their power to advocate for others, build bridges between conflicting parties, and create positive change in the world.

The integrated 8 is a powerful role model, inspiring others with their courage, compassion, and unwavering commitment to justice and fairness. They are not afraid to take risks, to challenge the status quo, and to fight for what they believe in, but they do so with a deep understanding of the needs and feelings of others.

The journey to integration is not always easy, but it is incredibly rewarding. By embracing the qualities of the 2, 8s can discover a deeper sense of purpose and fulfillment in their lives. They can become more authentic, compassionate, and connected to the world around them.

DISINTEGRATION TO 5: UNDERSTANDING THE RISKS OF WITHDRAWAL AND SUSPICION

The Enneagram isn't just about growth and integration; it also explores the potential pitfalls and challenges that each type faces when under stress. For the Enneagram 8, the path of disintegration leads to type 5, the Investigator. This is a journey into the depths of isolation, withdrawal, and suspicion, a stark contrast to the 8's usual assertiveness and outward focus.

Understanding this potential for disintegration is crucial for Eights, as it can help them to recognize the warning signs and take proactive steps to avoid falling into unhealthy patterns. It also provides valuable insights into the motivations and behaviors of 5s, which can be helpful for building stronger relationships with this enigmatic type.

The 8's Stress Response: Retreating into the Mind

When faced with overwhelming stress or challenges, Eights may unconsciously adopt the traits of the 5. They may become more withdrawn and introverted, seeking solace in solitude and introspection. They may also become more suspicious and guarded, questioning the motives of others and doubting their own abilities.

This shift can be disorienting for Eights, who are used to being in control and taking charge. They may feel like they are losing their edge, their confidence, and their ability to connect with others. This can lead to a downward spiral of isolation, resentment, and self-doubt.

The 5's Influence: Detachment and Analysis

The 5's influence on the 8's disintegration can be seen in their increasing detachment from the world and their tendency to overanalyze situations. They may become preoccupied with their own thoughts and feelings, losing touch with their instincts and their connection to others.

This analytical mindset can be helpful in some situations, allowing Eights to gain a deeper understanding of their problems and develop strategies for overcoming them. However, when taken to extremes, it can lead to paralysis by analysis, where the 8 becomes so overwhelmed by information and possibilities that they are unable to take action.

The Risks of Disintegration

The 8's disintegration to 5 can have serious consequences for their well-being and relationships. They may become increasingly isolated, withdrawing from loved ones and social activities. They may also become more cynical and distrusting, doubting the intentions of others and fearing betrayal.

This can create a self-fulfilling prophecy, as the 8's withdrawal and suspicion may push away the very people who could offer support and connection. It can also lead to a loss of confidence and a feeling of powerlessness, as the 8 feels increasingly unable to cope with the challenges they face.

Reversing the Disintegration Process

The good news is that disintegration is not a permanent state. By recognizing the warning signs and taking proactive steps, Eights can reverse the process and return to a more balanced and healthy state.

This involves:

- **Reconnecting with their gut center:** Eights need to re-engage with their instincts and intuition, trusting their gut feelings and taking decisive action.
- **Reaching out for support:** Eights need to break out of their isolation and seek connection with others. This can involve

talking to a trusted friend, therapist, or mentor, or simply spending time with loved ones.

- **Practicing self-compassion:** Eights need to be kind to themselves, recognizing that everyone struggles at times. They need to avoid self-criticism and negative self-talk, and focus on their strengths and accomplishments.
- **Embracing vulnerability:** Eights need to allow themselves to be vulnerable, to express their emotions, and to ask for help when needed. This can help them to build stronger relationships and foster a greater sense of connection and belonging.

By taking these steps, Eights can overcome their tendency towards disintegration and embrace a more integrated and fulfilling life. They can learn to balance their need for control with a willingness to trust others, and they can discover a deeper sense of connection and belonging.

Remember, the Enneagram is not about labeling or limiting yourself. It's about understanding your patterns, your strengths, and your challenges so that you can make conscious choices and live a more authentic and fulfilling life. By recognizing and addressing your potential for disintegration, you can unlock new levels of growth and transformation.

PERSONAL GROWTH STRATEGIES: TOOLS FOR SELF-AWARENESS AND TRANSFORMATION

Embarking on a journey of personal growth is a courageous endeavor for anyone, but for the Enneagram 8, it's a particularly transformative experience. Eights are often driven by a desire for self-improvement, seeking to harness their strengths, overcome their challenges, and live a more fulfilling life. However, their fear of vulnerability and need for control can sometimes create roadblocks on this path.

This chapter will explore a variety of personal growth strategies tailored specifically for the Enneagram 8. These strategies are designed to help Eights cultivate greater self-awareness, develop healthier coping mechanisms, and embrace a more balanced and integrated way of being.

1. Self-Reflection and Journaling

Self-reflection is a powerful tool for personal growth, allowing us to examine our thoughts, feelings, and behaviors with greater clarity and objectivity. For Eights, who often suppress their emotions or react impulsively, taking time for introspection can be incredibly valuable.

Journaling can be a helpful way to process emotions, identify patterns of behavior, and track progress over time. Eights can use journaling to explore their triggers, their fears, their desires, and their aspirations. They can also use it to reflect on their interactions with others, to gain insights into their strengths and weaknesses, and to develop a deeper understanding of themselves.

2. Mindfulness and Meditation

Mindfulness and meditation practices can help Eights to become more present and grounded in the moment. By focusing on their breath and bodily sensations, they can learn to calm their minds, reduce stress, and cultivate a greater sense of inner peace.

Mindfulness can also help Eights to become more aware of their emotional reactions, to identify triggers before they escalate, and to choose more constructive responses. Meditation can provide a safe space for Eights to explore their emotions without judgment or fear of vulnerability.

3. Therapy and Coaching

Working with a therapist or coach can provide Eights with a supportive and confidential space to explore their challenges, develop new coping mechanisms, and work towards their personal growth goals. A skilled professional can help Eights to identify their blind spots, challenge their limiting beliefs, and develop healthier ways of relating to themselves and others.

Therapy can also be a safe place for Eights to express their emotions, explore their vulnerabilities, and heal from past traumas. Coaching can help Eights to set goals, develop action plans, and stay motivated on their journey towards self-improvement.

4. Building Strong Relationships

Healthy relationships can be a powerful catalyst for personal growth, providing Eights with support, feedback, and opportunities for self-reflection. By surrounding themselves with people who love and accept them for who they are, Eights can learn to trust others, to let down their guard, and to embrace their vulnerability.

Intimate relationships can be particularly transformative for Eights, as they offer a safe space to explore their emotions, to practice vulnerability, and to develop a deeper understanding of themselves. Friendships can also be valuable, providing Eights with a sense of community, belonging, and support.

5. Embracing Creative Expression

Creative expression can be a powerful outlet for Eights to channel their emotions, explore their inner world, and connect with their deeper selves. Whether it's through writing, painting, music, dance, or any other form of creative expression, Eights can find a way to express their feelings in a safe and constructive way.

Creative expression can also help Eights to develop greater self-awareness and compassion. By exploring their emotions through art, they can gain a deeper understanding of their motivations, fears, and desires. They can also learn to see the world from different perspectives, to appreciate the beauty and complexity of human experience.

6. Engaging in Meaningful Work

Eights thrive on challenge, responsibility, and the opportunity to make a difference in the world. Engaging in meaningful work that aligns with their values and passions can be a powerful motivator for personal growth.

By using their strengths to serve others, Eights can develop a greater sense of purpose and fulfillment. They can also learn to channel their energy into constructive action, rather than using it to dominate or control others.

Meaningful work can also provide Eights with opportunities to collaborate with others, to learn from different perspectives, and to develop a more collaborative and inclusive approach to leadership.

The Journey of a Lifetime

Personal growth is not a destination but a lifelong journey. For the Enneagram 8, this journey involves embracing vulnerability, cultivating empathy, and developing a more balanced and integrated way of being. It's a journey that requires courage, honesty, and a willingness to step outside of one's comfort zone. But the rewards are immeasurable.

By embracing personal growth, Eights can discover a deeper sense of purpose, fulfillment, and joy in their lives. They can become more authentic, compassionate, and connected to the world around them. They can unleash their full potential and live a life that is both powerful and meaningful.

EMBRACING YOUR CHALLENGER SPIRIT: LEADING WITH STRENGTH, AUTHENTICITY, AND COMPASSION

As we conclude our exploration of the Enneagram 8, it's time to celebrate the unique power and potential that lies within the Challenger spirit. Eights are a force to be reckoned with – passionate, driven, and fiercely committed to their values. They are natural leaders, advocates, and protectors, with a remarkable ability to inspire and motivate others.

Embracing your Challenger spirit means recognizing and honoring your strengths while also acknowledging your vulnerabilities and areas for growth. It means accepting your full range of emotions, from anger to tenderness, and learning to express them in healthy ways. It means using your power for good, advocating for justice, and fighting for what you believe in, while also practicing compassion and empathy.

Leading with Strength and Authenticity

Eights are born leaders. They have a natural charisma and confidence that draws others to them. They are decisive, action-oriented, and unafraid to take risks. They inspire others with their vision, their passion, and their unwavering belief in themselves.

However, true leadership is not about dominance or control. It's about empowering others, fostering collaboration, and creating a shared vision for the future. Eights can embrace their leadership potential by learning to listen to others, to value diverse perspectives, and to create an environment where everyone feels safe to speak their truth.

Authenticity is another key component of effective leadership.

Eights are at their best when they are true to themselves, when they speak their minds, and when they act in accordance with their values. By embracing their authenticity, Eights can inspire others to do the same, creating a culture of honesty, integrity, and trust.

Cultivating Compassion and Empathy

While Eights are often seen as tough and assertive, they also have a deep capacity for compassion and empathy. They are fiercely loyal to their loved ones and fiercely protective of those they consider their own.

However, Eights may struggle to express their softer emotions, fearing that vulnerability will make them weak or susceptible to harm. By embracing their vulnerability and learning to express their emotions in healthy ways, Eights can cultivate greater compassion for themselves and others.

Empathy is another crucial skill for Eights to develop. By learning to see the world through the eyes of others, they can gain a deeper understanding of their motivations, fears, and desires. This can lead to more meaningful connections, better communication, and a more compassionate approach to life.

Living a Life of Purpose and Passion

Eights are passionate individuals with a strong sense of purpose. They are driven to make a difference in the world, to leave their mark, and to create a legacy that will endure.

By aligning their actions with their values and passions, Eights can live a life that is both fulfilling and meaningful. They can use their strengths to make a positive impact on the world, to advocate for justice, and to fight for what they believe in.

Living a life of purpose also involves taking care of oneself. Eights need to prioritize their own well-being, to ensure that they have the energy and resilience to continue their journey. This can involve setting boundaries, practicing self-care, and seeking support when needed.

The Challenger's Legacy

Eights are a powerful force for good in the world. Their courage, conviction, and unwavering belief in themselves can inspire others to reach their full potential. By embracing their strengths, overcoming their challenges, and living a life of purpose and passion, Eights can leave a lasting legacy that will continue to inspire generations to come.

The journey of the Enneagram 8 is one of continuous growth and transformation. By embracing their full potential, Eights can become true leaders, compassionate advocates, and inspiring role models for others. They can live a life that is both powerful and meaningful, a life that is truly aligned with their deepest values and aspirations.